John Corbet

A second discourse of the religion of England

John Corbet

A second discourse of the religion of England

ISBN/EAN: 9783337274856

Printed in Europe, USA, Canada, Australia, Japan

Cover: Foto ©Lupo / pixelio.de

More available books at **www.hansebooks.com**

A

Second Discourse

OF THE

RELIGION

OF

ENGLAND:

Further Asserting,

That Reformed Christianity,
Setled in its Due Latitude, is the Stability and
Advancement of this KINGDOM.

Wherein is included,

An ANSWER to a late Book,

ENTITULED,

A Discourse of TOLERATION.

LONDON, Printed in the Year 1668.

A Second

DISCOURSE

OF THE

RELIGION of *ENGLAND*.

SECT. I.

Of the Foundation of our Peace already laid in the Religion of the Nation, and the Structure thereof, to be perfected by the Unity of that Profession.

Concerning Religion in this Kingdom, there have been, and still are great thoughts of heart, and the troubled state thereof hath much disturbed the Minds of Men, and the whole course of Human Affairs. Doubtless, Religion it self is not in fault, which in its right and sound state, being an Institution holy, just and good, must needs be of great efficacy to compose and quiet our minds, and to heal and settle the Nations. But that which in it self is Excellent, is by the Errors and Corruptions of men, made subject to much vanity. And the Adver-

fary

fary of Mankind being not able to raze out the deep impreſ-
ſions thereof that are in our Nature, hath made it his Maſter-
piece ſo to corrupt or diſcompoſe it, as to diſorder the Paſſi-
ons of Men, and the Affairs of the World about it.

Concerning the Cure of theſe Diſtempers, and the Re-
dreſs of the Evils thence ariſing, there is no cauſe of Deſpair
or Deſpondency, if Men ceaſe from their high Provocations, and God from his righteous Indignation. The moſt
effectual means of Reconciliation between the Diſagree-
ing Parties, is, For all of them to be reconciled to God.
Then would that Spirit of Perverſneſs, which by the Divine
Diſpleaſure hath been mingled in the midſt of us, be con-
troled and vanquiſhed ; and Offences and Prejudices being
removed, we might diſcern the Way of Peace. God for-
bid that Sentence ſhould paſs upon this Generation, *De-*
ſtruction and miſery is in their paths, and the way of peace they
have not known.

Next, under the Divine Favour and Bleſſing, our Help
ſtandeth in the Wiſdom and Piety of our SOVEREIGN
and His PARLIAMENT. But this Grand Affair is acknowledged to be full of difficulties, cauſed by the Paſſi-
ons, Prejudices and Intereſts of the ſeveral Parties. Ne-
vertheleſs, the Prudence and Patience of thoſe that ſit at
the Helm of Government, is able to Maſter it : For, the
Ground-work of Peace is laid to their hands, in the Religion of the Nation ; and the Impartial may deſcry the oppor-
tunity of ſuch a Settlement as may accommodate all thoſe
Parties in which the Nation's Peace is bound up.

The true Intereſt of Soveraignty, is the ſelf-ſame with
that of the Univerſality, or whole Body of the Kingdom;
and this is founded in ſuch a Common-Good, as belongs to
all ſorts of men, by whom the Publike Weal conſiſts. And
where there are, and inevitably will be different Perſwaſions among them, the Wiſdom of the Government is to contract

tract and leſſen their differences, as much as it is poſſible; but, howſoever, to prevent or heal diviſions, and to hold them united among themſelves, in the common Benefit, and all of them neceſſarily dependant upon the State. This is a firm Baſis of the perpetual ſtability of Empire, as alſo of the Subjects Tranquility and Proſperity; and the preſent Diſcourſe reſts upon this Principle as its ſure Foundation.

Now in this Realm, the joint Stock of thoſe ſeveral Parties, for matter of Religion, is *REFORMED CHRISTIANITY*, for which they are all jealous, even unto diſcompoſure, upon any Encroachments of the Popiſh Party. Wherefore, it is the Wiſdom of this Government, to remove or leſſen the Differences, and to cure the Diviſions which now diſturb and divide the Proteſtants, and to hold them united among themſelves, and all of them in firm dependance upon this State, and conſequently, to give them all their due encouragement, not indeed in looſe and irregular wayes, but in a ruled Order, conſiſtent with ſtable Polity, and agreeable to the Government of this Kingdom.

The Ground-work being already laid in the Proteſtant Religion, which is the general and grand Intereſt of this Nation, the Structure and Fabrick of the Unity and Peace of this Realm, is more or leſs perfected, as the Unity of this Profeſſion, and the Peace and Concord of its Profeſſors, is more or leſs acquired. And now this great Queſtion lyes before us, *Whether the Unity of Religion be obtained by requiring a Conformity of Judgment and Practice in matters of perpetual difference from the beginning of the Reformation unto this very day; or, by permitting a latitude of Opinion and Practice in thoſe points; and that not infinite and inordinate, but limited by the Publike Rule.*

SECT.

SECT. II.

The Good of the several Parties is best secured by common Equity, and the good of the Universality.

HOw happy might the disposition of Human Affairs be, if that were acknowledged in mens Practice, which is most clear and obvious to Human Understanding, *That things of common Equity and regard to all sorts, who are necessarily included in the Publike State, be preferred by each particular Party, before great Advantages to themselves apart, with disregard of all others.* For, all particular Interests which are uncorrupt, and will hold firm, are imbarked in the Interest of the Universality, and must sink or swim therewith: Whereupon, not onely the Commonwealth, but the more appropriate Concernments of men, are better secured for continuance, by this Moderation and common Equity.

There lye before us the Protestant Religion, (which is the true Primitive Christianity) and the Ancient, Equal and Happy Constitution of the Government of this Kingdom. The Conservation and Advancement of both These, are infinitely more valuable than the prevalence of Parties, by all true Protestants, and true *English* men. A publike Spirit is that which is truly pious and generous. But, over and above this Noble and Christian Consideration, this also should be very prevalent, That those Two great things before named, in which all do share, and by which all subsist, are the Basis even of the more private and contracted Benefits of the several Parties; and by disturbing these, they weaken their own hold, and disturb their own safety. Those that hate Moderation, and follow Extremes on either hand, consider not the true state of *England*. It is an unhappy Error when divided Parties, who when all is done,

done, in their divided state, can be but Parties, and not the Whole, shall so act in their turns, as if they took themselves to be the whole Body of the Nation, or equivalent thereunto. And it is a calamitous averseness, when such as must live together either as Friends or Enemies, shall refuse lawful and safe terms of mutual agreement.

As for Conscience, and its high Concernments, if it be guided by that *Wisdom which is from above, which is first pure, then peaceable*, it puts in no caution against the healing of this breach : For, Order and Peace may be obtained upon terms not repugnant to the Principles of either Party. His Majesty's Wisdom hath rightly comprehended this matter, in His Declaration concerning Ecclesiastical Affairs, where He saith, " *We are the rather indu-* " *ced to take this upon Us*, (that is, to give some deter- " mination to the matters in difference) *by finding upon a* " *full Conference that we have had with the Learned men of* " *several Perswasions, That the Mischiefs under which both* " *Church and State do at present suffer, do not result from* " *any formed Doctrine or Conclusion which either Party* " *maintains or avows; but from the Passion, Appetite, and* " *Interest of particular persons, which contract greater pre-* " *judice to each other by those Affections, than would natu-* " *rally arise from their Opinions.* It is apparent, that the avowed Doctrines on either side, could not set the Parties at this distance, if their Spirits and Interests were reconciled.

SECT. III.

What may be esteemed a good Constitution of the State Ecclesiastical.

AS concerning the publike Order, it imports exceedingly to discern and make a difference between things desirable, but morally impossible, or extreamly impro-

improbable, and things neceſſary and attainable. Perfect unanimity about matters of Religion, and a harmony of Opinion in all Theological Truths, is very deſirable; but it was never yet found in any Age of the World, among thoſe that owned the ſame Religion, and conſequently it cannot be neceſſary in all thoſe that ought to be comprehended in the ſame Church, or Religious Communion. For which cauſe, a preciſe Uniformity in matters of meer Opinion, will hardly ever paſs with general ſatisfaction: Neither is it of that importance, that ſome make it to be, for Peace and Edification. There is another thing not onely deſirable, but the indiſpenſable duty of all particular perſons, which is Brotherly Love among all that receive *the common Faith once given to the Saints.* This is of far greater conſequence than the former, and more largely attainable, becauſe it is a Catholick Diſpoſition, and the right Spirit of true Chriſtianity; and indeed, the failing hereof is lamentable and reproachful. Howbeit, this excellent Chriſtian Vertue is commonly much interrupted and impaired in many, by prejudicate Opinions, and depraved Affections; and it muſt not be expected, but that Animoſities and Jealouſies may remain between men of different Perſwaſions, by reaſon of the corruption of man's nature, and the infirmities of the beſt of men. And therefore the foundation of a ſolid National Settlement, muſt not, and need not be laid in mens good diſpoſitions and inclinations: For, although the diſtemper of many minds continue, yet publike Order, and ſteddy Government, is in no wiſe impoſſible.

Things are neceſſary, either as the End, or the Means. The things here conſidered, that are neceſſary as the End, are, The Advancement of the Proteſtant Religion, and the Kingdom of *England*, the Tranquility of Church and State, and the Security of all ſound Proteſtants, and good Subjects.

Subjects. That which is necessary as the Means, is the Publike Rule and Standard by which these blessed Ends may be obtained; that, notwithstanding the remainder of mens Perversness, the common high Concerns of Reformed Religion, and of this Kingdom, be not disturbed, impaired, or cast back by the Altercations that may chance to arise between men of different private Opinions, and different partial Interests. The high Importance and Necessity of a stated Rule of such Force and Efficacy, evinceth the possibility thereof: For, so Noble and Necessary Ends, cannot be destitute of all possible Means leading thereunto. Evil Dispositions and Manners are the rise of Good Laws: And Law-makers, that are subject to like passions with other men, have the Wisdom to limit themselves and others, for the Universal Good, wherein the good of every Individual is secured.

The Publike Rule being to be framed to the proportion of the People that are to be setled under it, the chief regard must be had to their fixed and unmovable Perswasions and Inclinations, lest They should break the Rule, or the Rule break them. In a Nation whose Active Part is zealous of Religion, and able to discern, and addicted to discourse the Grounds thereof, the Order of Things ought, in the first place, to be directed to the satisfying of the Just and Reasonable Demands of Conscience, which being troubled, is a restless thing; and then to the outward Incouragements of Piety and Learning, and withall, to the bridling of Ambition, Avarice, Faction, and all depraved Appetite. It must be expected, That divers Obliquities and Deficiencies may remain, and Troubles will arise: but if that which is Wholesom and Good, be so predominant as to Master the Evils, though not to extinguish them, it is to be esteemed a Good Constitution.

SECT.

SECT. IV.

The Comprehensiveness of the Establishment, and the Allowance of a just Latitude of Dissents, is the best Remedy against Dissentions:

THere was lately published a Discourse for a due Latitude in Religion, by Comprehension, Toleration and Connivence, directed to this End, That the occasions of those Discords which divide the Members, and distract the whole Body of the Protestant Profession, might cease; and that the common Concernments, wherein the disagreeing Parties have a large joint Stock in things of greatest moment, might be pursued. This is encountred with an adverse Discourse, which is here to be examined, and the state and reason of the aforesaid Latitude, is to be further cleared.

Toleration being commonly understood of the permission of different ways of Religion, without the Line of the Approved Way, *A Discourse of Toleration* doth not hit *the Discourse of the Religion of England*, in the main thereof, whose chief Design is the Extension of the Established Order, and the Moderation therein required; and then Toleration is treated of analogically, with respect not only to common Charity, but to the Safety of the setled Polity. It is no less besides the mark, to argue from the Mischiefs of a boundless and licentious Toleration, against that which is Limited and well Managed, and hath for the Subject thereof, nothing that is intolerable.

But, if under this Name be comprehended also the Permission of diversity of Opinion in the same Established Order, let it be considered, Whether any ample Polity can consist without such Permission. For, it is a thing utterly unknown, and seems morally impossible, for any
numerous

numerous Society of Inquiring men, to be of the same judgment in all points of Religion. And though the *Sons of the Church*, as they are called, agree in those points wherein they all differ from the *Nonconformists*, yet they differ among themselves in far weightier Matters, and such as have caused great Schisms, and have been the subjects of the Debates and Determinations of some Synods in the Reformed Churches. Now if Charity among themselves, and their appropriate Interest, dispose them to this mutual forbearance, a more extensive Charity, and the common Interest of Reformed Christianity, should incline them to a forbearance in those other matters.

There is yet a greater Error committed about *the Subject of Toleration*, which the *Answerer*, by mistake, will have to be *Dissentions in Religion*, but is nothing so in the design of that Discourse to which he pretends an Answer. And this hath brought forth a large Impertinency, which takes up more than a third part of his Book: For, those whose Liberty He seeks to withstand, are not touched with that which he writes at large of the nature of Dissentions, with their Causes and Consequences, and the Magistrates duty concerning them, whether it be right or wrong, setting aside the injurious application thereof. And all that labour had been spared, if he had put a difference between *Dissention* and *Dissent*, words that are near in sound, and perhaps, sometimes, promiscuously used; but in their strict and proper sense, far distant: For, *Dissention* is no sooner presented to the mind, but it is apprehended as something either culpable and offensive, or calamitous and unhappy: But *Dissent* is of a better notion, and is not necessarily on both sides, either a Fault or a Grievance. But if this Author means by Dissentions, no more then dissents or differences of Opinion, with what truth and justice can he charge them all (as he doth) with such execrable Causes

and

and Effects. Diffentions have been, and may be remedied, and their fuel being taken away, thofe flames will be extinguifhed: But diverfity of Opinion feems in this ftate of Human Nature, to be irremediable. It is therefore hoped, that the ftate of this Church and Kingdom is not fo deplorable, as to want a Settlement while thefe Diffents remain. Moreover, there are private diffents between particular men, within the latitude of the Publike Rule; and there are diffents that may be called Publike, as being from the Publike Rule, or fome parts thereof. Now the broader and more comprehenfive the Rule is, the fewer will be the Diffenters from it. And the permiffion of private diverfities of Opinion, in a juft Latitude within the Rule, is the means to leffen Publike Diffents, and confequently, Diffentions much more. And this was the main fcope of the firft *Difcourfe*.

The great importance of *Unity in the Church of Chrift*, is acknowledged and contended for as much on this fide, as on the other: Howbeit, we do not believe that Chrift our Head hath laid the Confervation and Unity of His Church, upon unwritten and unneceffary Doctrines, and little Opinions, and Sacred Rites and Ceremonies of meer Human Tradition and Inftitution. But He hath fet out the Rule and Meafure of Unity in fuch fort, as that upon Diffents in thofe things, the Members of this Society might not break into Schifms, to a mutual condemnation and abhorrency. The impofing of fuch things (except in thofe Ages whofe Blindnefs and Barbarifm difpofed them to ftupidity and grofs fecurity in their Religion) hath been ever found to break Unity, and to deftroy, or much impair Charity, Goodnefs, Meeknefs, and Patience, which are Vital Parts, and chief Excellencies of Chriftianity.

SECT.

SECT. V.

Whether the prefent Diffentions are but fo many Factions in the State.

ONE grand Objection is, *That the Diffentions among us, are but fo many feveral Factions in the State.* But, meer diffents in Religion, are no State-Factions at all, but proceed from a more lafting Caufe, than particular Defigns, or any temporary Occafions, even from the incurable Infirmity of our Nature. And if it were granted, That the Diffentions were State-Factions; yet, they are not fo originally and radically, but by accident. Some may take advantage to raife and keep up Factions by them. For this caufe, take out of the way the ftumbling-block of needlefs rigors, and then Diffentions will ceafe or languifh, and confequently, the State Factions (if there be any fuch that are kept up by them) will come to nothing.

It is fo evident, that *Toleration*, which came not in till after the breach between the Late King and Parliament, *did not open the avenues to our Miferies*, that one may wonder any fhould fay it did. But, meet Indulgence to all found Proteftants, is the likelieft means of ftopping fuch avenues. And, *if it be for the Intereft of England to have no Factions*, the beft way is to remove thofe burdens, which, like a partition-wall, hath kept afunder the Profeffors of the fame Religion: Then *the Mafters of our Troubles.* (whofoever they be) *cannot have that advantage by their Eminency in their Parties, to drive on their Defigns in the State.* Factious Spirits are difappointed, when Honeft Minds are fatisfied and fecured.

This Author relates the Aims of feveral Parties on this manner: *The Papifts are for the Supremacy of the Bifhop of Rome; fome of the other Sects are for a Commonwealth;*
others.

others are for the Fift Monarchy. But, if the true ſtate of the *Nonconformiſts* be well conſidered, it will be found, that in Them, as well as any others, the King and Kingdom is concerned, and the good of Both promoted. It is not with them, as with the Popiſh Party, who have ſuch a ſevered Intereſt to themſelves, that the State is little concerned in it, ſave onely to beware of its Incroachments. But the Proteſtant Diſſenters, are ſuch as do much of the Buſineſs of the Nation, and have not their Intereſt apart, but in ſtrict conjunction with the whole Body-Politick. Yea, they have no poſſible means of enſuring their Intereſt, but by Legal-Security obtained from the Higher Power, and by comporting with the general tranquility both of the Church and State of *England.* They cannot flye to the Refuge of any Foreign Prince or State, (as the *Papiſts* have done frequently) they acknowledg no Foreign Juriſdiction, (which is a Principle of the *Popiſh Faith*) but all their Stake lies at home, and they can have no ſure Hold that is aliene from the Happineſs of the King and Kingdom. An Impartial Obſerver cannot but diſcern this. If it be lawful to name a thing ſo much to be abhorred, as a Change of the Ancient Laws and Government, they could not be happy, nor do their Work by ſuch an unhappy Change. Experience witneſſeth, That their Intereſt is not for haſty and unſtable Victory, or unfixed Liberty; but, for a ſtate of firm Conſiſtence and Security; and that they cannot hold their own, but by the common Safety both of Prince and People.

The ſumm of this Matter is, That a Party not onely comporting with the good Eſtate of this Realm, but even ſubſiſting by it, and therefore firmly linked unto it, ſhould not be caſt off.

SECT. VI.

Whether the NONCONFORMISTS Principles tend to Sects and Schifms.

SOme Reafons were offered to fhew, That Indulgence towards Diffenting Proteftants, did much concern the Peace and Happinefs of this Realm. And the Prudent will judg Arguments of that fort to be of the greateft weight in the Affairs of Government. There is no need to reinforce the cogency of thofe Reafons : The Adverfary hath wrefted them to an odious meaning, contrary to their manifeft true intent; but whether he hath indeed evinced them to be of little or no moment; or, whether they ftand in full force, let judicious men confider. The whole reafoning in that particular, refts upon this Maxime, That it is the SOVEREIGN's true Intereft, to make his divided People to be one among themfelves, and to keep them all in dependance upon Himfelf, as the Procurer of their common fafety.

The Prejudices that have been conceived, and the Calumnies that have been raifed againft the *Nonconformifts*, gave occafion of refolving this Queftion, *Whether they be of a judgment and temper that makes them capable of being brought under the Magiftrates Paternal Care and Conduct, to fuch a ftated Order as will comport with this Church and Kingdom ?* This, by the *Anfwerer*, is termed *a Dialect of Canting*, and is wilfully wrefted into a Queftion of another nature. Whether he had occafion given him to fpeak fo fcornfully, let any judg that underftand fober language. But, that they might appear uncapable of a Comprehenfion, he fticks not to affirm, *That the Principles of Presbyterian Perfwafion, do not admit of any ftability, but may be drawn out to patronize the wildeft Sects that are or have been.* And his
main

main proof is taken from the bare word of Two of their Eminent Adverſaries. He might have remembred, That the ſame Reproach is caſt upon the Principles of *Proteſtan-tiſm*, by *Romiſh* Writers. One may well ask, Where is the Truth and Candor of thoſe men that write after this manner? Conſider the *French, Dutch, Helvetian* Churches, how intire they keep themſelves in Orthodox Unity, from the Gangrene of Sects and Schiſms. The Church of *Scotland*, whilſt it was *Presbyterian*, was inferior to none in the Unity of Doctrine and Church-Communion. Did *Prelacy* ever effect the like Unity in the Church of *England*? And ſhall the Sects that now are, or lately were in this Nation, be charged upon *Presbytery*, that was never ſetled among us, and againſt which the Sectaries had the greateſt indignation? Though that Way never obtained in *England*, nor was favoured with the Magiſtrates vigorous aid, yet it is very untrue, *that the firſt admirers and friends thereof, grew ſick of it, and hiſſed for the other Sects to affront, reproach and baffle it.* It is well known, that it received thoſe diſgraces from another ſort of men.

The aſſerting of this Government, is far from the deſign of this or the former Treatiſe; yet it may be lawful to vindicate it from unjuſt aſperſions. The *Anſwerer* is pleaſed to ſtile it, *No other but a Sect.* I hope he doth not intend to make the Foreign Reformed Churches, but ſo many Combinations of Sectaries. If his meaning be, that is no better than a Sect in *England*, *becauſe another Government is eſtabliſhed by Law*, let him tell us, Whether *Epiſcopacy* would be a Sect, if it ſhould appear in thoſe Countries where *Presbytery* is the Legal Government? No leſs will follow, if the Notion of Sect be extended ſo far, as to fetch in whatſoever diſſents from the Order by Law eſtabliſhed.

SECT.

SECT. VII.

Of their Principles touching OBEDIENCE *and* GOVERNMENT.

ANother great Prejudice taken up againſt the *Noncon-formiſts*, is, That they are inconſiſtent with any Regular Government: And this Author reports, that it is a common Maxime among the Diſſenters, *That an Indifferent Thing becomes Vnlawful by being Commanded.* But let the World hear them ſpeak for themſelves out of their *Account to His Majeſty concerning the Review and Alteration of the Liturgy.*

" We humbly beſeech Your Majeſty to believe, That
" we own no Principles of Faction or Diſobedience, nor
" patronize the Errors or Obſtinacy of any. It is granted
" us by all, That nothing ſhould be commanded us by man,
" which is contrary to the Word of God: That, if it be,
" and we know it, we are bound not to perform it, God
" being the Abſolute Univerſal Sovereign: That we muſt
" uſe all juſt means to diſcern the Will of God, and whe-
" ther the Commands of Men be contrary to it: That, if
" the Command be ſinful, and any through neglect of ſuf-
" ficient ſearch, ſhould judg it Lawful, his culpable Error
" excuſeth not his doing it, from being ſin: And there-
" fore as a reaſonable creature muſt needs have a judg-
" ment of diſcerning, that he may rationally obey it;
" ſo is he with the greateſt care and diligence, to exerciſe it
" in the greateſt things, even the obeying of God, and the
" ſaving of his Soul: And that where a ſtrong probability
" of a great Sin and Danger lieth before us, we muſt not
" raſhly run on without ſearch: And that to go on againſt
" Conſcience where it is miſtaken, is ſin and danger to him
" that erreth. And on the other ſide, we are remembred,

C   that

" that in things no way against the Law of God, the Com-
" mands of our Governors must be obeyed ; but if they
" command what God forbids, we must patiently submit
" to suffering, and every soul must be subject to the Higher
" Powers for Conscience sake, and not resist : The Pub-
" like Judgment, Civil or Ecclesiastical, belongeth only
" to publike persons, and not to any private man : That
" no man must be causlesly or pragmatically inquisitive
" into the reasons of his Superiors .Commands ; nor by
" Pride and Self-conceitedness, exalt his own understand-
" ing above its Worth and Office ; but all to be modestly
" and humbly self-suspicious : That none must erroneously
" pretend to God's Law, against the just Command of his
" Superiors, nor pretend the doing of his duty to be a sin :
" That he who suspecteth his Superiors Commands to be
" against Gods Laws, must use all means for full informa-
" tion, before he settle in a course of disobeying them :
" And that he who indeed discovereth any thing comman-
" ded, to be a sin ; though he must not do it, must manage
" his Opinion with very great care and tenderness of the
" Publike Peace, and the honour of his Governors. These
" are our Principles : If we are otherwise represented to
" Your Majesty, we are mis-represented : If we are accu-
" sed of contradicting them, we humbly crave that we may
" not be condemned before we be heard.

This is sound speech that cannot be reproved. Wherefore if the Clemency of their Superiors shall remit those
Injunctions that may wellbe dispensed with, and unto which
they cannot yeeld conformity for fear lest they sin against
God ; their Principles will dispose them with an humble
and thankful acquiescence, to receive so great a Benefit.

SECT. VIII.

Of placing them in the same rank for Crime and Guilt, with the PAPISTS.

THE *Answerer* hath not feared to set the *Papists*, and the *Protestant Dissenters*, upon the same level, in the guilt of Rebellion, Cruelty and Turbulency. For a high Charge having been made good against *Popery*, *That it disposeth Subjects to Rebellion: That it persecutes all other Religions within its reach: That wheresoever it finds encouragement, it is restless, till it bear down all, or hath put all in disorder:* He comes and tells the World, That the *Nonconformists are no more innocent of the same Crimes.* Can men of sound minds and temperate spirits, believe this? And what greater advantage can be given the *Popish Party*, then that a *Protestant Writer* should declare and publish, that so great a part of *Protestants* are equally involved with them in those heinous Crimes with which the *Protestants* have always charged them? And that such a one should tell them, *That it will seem unequal to deny a Toleration to them, and grant it unto others that are here pleaded for;* which is in effect to say, They have as good reason to expect an Indulgence from this State, as others that maintain the Doctrine of the Church of *England*, yea, such as communicate in her publike Worship. Is there no better way of exalting *Prelacy*, and disgracing its supposed Adversaries, then by this Reproach and Damage done to the whole *Protestant* Profession? Yea, he so far extenuates the guilt of *Papists*, and brings it down so low, as to make it common to all other Sects. In which one would think he should have been more wary, who in one place stretcheth the notion of *Sect* so far, as to make its reason to lye in being different from the Established Form of Church Government. Now

for

for matter of practice, he imputes the same guilt to all other
Sects; *And if the Papists* (faith he) *have any Doctrines
which countenance those Practises, that is to be accounted as
the issue of their insolency in their own greatness.* And he implies, That it is onely the want of strength, that other
Sects are not so bad as they for such kind of Doctrine, as
well as Practice.   Such passages falling from a *Protestants*
Pen, may do the *Papists* better service than their late Apo-
logy. But why doth he say, *If the Papists have any such
Doctrines?* Doth he not know they have? The Church of
England was assured of it, when concerning the Adherents
of *Rome*, she used this expression in a publike form of
Prayer, *Whose Religion is Rebellion, and whose Faith is Faction.* We wish their eyes were open, who cannot see more
permanent and effectual causes of the aforesaid Crimes pe-
culiar to that Religion, and rooted in the Principles thereof. The evidence hereof given in the former *Discourse,*
is not needful to be reherfed in this place.

This Author (as others that oppose the wayes of Amity
and Peace) loves to grate upon a string that sounds harsh,
To renew the remembrance of the late Warr. Those di-
stracted Times, are the great Storehouse and Armory, out
of which such men do fetch their Weapons of offence;
and the great Strong-hold, unto which they always retreat
when they are vanquished by the force of Reason, and
then they think they are safe, though therein they contra-
dict the true intent of the Act of Oblivion. Some of those
that now so importunately urge the Injury and Tyranny
of those Times, did then sufficiently comply with Usur-
pers, and left *Episcopacy* to sink or swim; and did partake
of the chiefest Favours and Preferments that were then
conferred. And on the other hand, such as they upbraid,
and are now Sufferers, did as little comply with those that
subverted the Government, and did as zealously appear
for

for the rescue of our late Sovereign, and for the restitution
of His present Majesty, as any sort of men in the Realm.
But to intermeddle in the Differences of those Times, and
to repeat Odious Matters, and to use Recriminations that
will disturb the minds of men, and tend to a perpetual Mis-
chief, is aliene from, and opposite unto my Pacifick Endea-
vours. As for his charging the *Nonconformists* with certain
Doctrines and Positions by him there mentioned (which I
know none that maintains) and other Accusations and Reports relating to the time of the Warr ; the Truth or Fals-
hood, the Equity or Iniquity, the Candor or Disingenuity
of his Testimony in those things, is left to the judgment of
the Righteous God, and of Impartial Men.

SECT. IX.

Whether their Inconformity be Conscientious or Wilful.

ANother part of the Proceeding is very Unrighteous
and Presumptuous. The Dissenting Ministers appeal
to God, That they dare not Conform for Conscience sake.
This Author hence inferrs, *The force of the Argument is,
There is a Necessity of Toleration, because they Will not conform.* Is a *Cannot for Conscience sake*, of no more force than
a bare *Will not?* But who best knows their hearts, themselves
or their Adversaries? He would make the world believe,
that not Conscience, but Obstinacy and Faction, is the
cause of their holding out, *and that the greatest part were
trapann'd into Nonconformity.* That trifling story of their
being trapann'd, is not worthy of serious discourse. It is so
evident, as not to be denied, That about the time the Act of
Uniformity was to be put in practice, there were motions
and overtures of Indulgence from the King and some of the
great Officers of State, who were known to have high affection and esteem for the Church of *England*, yet did ap-
prove

prove and promote thofe Overtures as the beft Expedient
for the fetling of this Church and Kingdom. But to let
that pafs, Can men of Underftanding and Candor think,
that fo many ferious perfons, who as well as others, may be
thought to love themfelves, their Families and Relations,
fhould continue fuch egregioufly obftinate Fools, as to re-
fufe the Comforts of their Temporal Being, for a Humor,
and remain in a ftate of Deprivation, into which they had
been meerly trapann'd? As for the objected *unprofitable-*
nefs of their returning, how doth it appear? What hinders
their Capacity of gaining Benefices, yea and Dignities, if
they could Conform? Why fhould they not find as good
acceptation as others, in their Preaching and Converfation?
It may be they would enter too faft, for the good liking of
fome, into thofe Preferments, who therefore would fet fuch
Barrs againft them, as they fhould not be able to break tho-.
rough.

SECT. X.

Of their peaceable Inclinations, and readinefs to be fa-
tisfied.

IN the late Times of Ufurpation, there were apparent
predifpofitions in this fort of men to Peace and Concord.
The longing defire and expectation that was in them, as
much as in any others, of a National Settlement, and general Compofure, did accelerate His Majefty's Peaceable
Reftauration. Surely they were not fo ftupid as to imagine that great Turn of Affairs, without the thoughts of
their own yeilding, and fuch as they hoped would be effectual with thofe of the other Perfwafion. Their early and
ready Overtures of Reconciliation, which are publikely
made known, will teftifie their Moderation, to the prefent
and future Ages. Their Offers of Acquiefcing in *Epifcopacy*
Regulated, and the *Liturgy* Reformed, was on their part, a
goed

good advance towards Union. His Majesty hath given this Testimony of them in His Declaration : *When We were in Holland , We were attended by many Grave and Learned Ministers from hence, who were looked upon as the most able and principal Assertors of the* Presbyterian *Opinions , with whom We had as much Conference as the multitude of Affairs which were then upon Us, would permit Us to have; and to Our great Satisfaction and Comfort , found them persons full of Affection to Us., of Zeal for the Peace of the Church and State , and neither Enemies (as they had been given out to be)to* Episcopacy *or* Liturgy*,but modestly to desire such alterations as without shaking Foundations , might best allay the present Distempers which the indisposition of the Time , and the tenderness of some mens Consciences had contracted.*

I wonder at the confidence of that Assertion in the *Answer , That it is sufficiently known , That none of the present Nonconformists did in the least measure agree in the use of those little things; and though desired by the King to read so much of the Liturgy as themselves had not exception against , and so could have no pretence from Conscience.* For it is well known, that some of them did in compliance with the Kings desire, read part of the Liturgy in their Churches. As for others that did not, perhaps for the prevention of scandal they might use their liberty of forbearance till some Reformation were obtained. The truth is, the Concessions on this side have been abused, to the reproach and disadvantage of the depressed Party; and from their readiness to yeild so far as they can, for the common peace sake, a perverse inference is made, That they might yeild throughout, if Humor and Faction did not rule them. Is there any Justice or Charity in such dealing? May not men of upright Consciences, and peaceable Inclinations , forbear the insisting upon some things to them very desirable, and give place to some things not approved by them as the best in that kind,

if

if so be they might obtain their Peace and Liberty , by Indulgence granted them in other things, wherein Conscience binds them up that they cannot yeild? Moreover, some Concessions made by particular men of very Catholick spirits, in the earnest pursuit of Peace, have been wrack'd and wrested to a sense beyond their true import; and then they that so handle them, triumph in their own conceit, over them, as if they had given up the whole Cause. Certasnly they are ill employed, who from their Brethrens yeelding offers, raise Opposition against them, and endeavour to set them further off.

SECT. XI.

The propounded Latitude leaves out nothing necessary to secure the Church's Peace.

TO set forth the propounded Latitude in the particular Limits thereof, is not agreeable to a Discourse of this nature: For it were presumptuous both in reference to Superiors, and to the Party concerned in it. And it is unnecessary; for Prejudices being removed, and the Conveniency of a greater Latitude being acknowledged, the particular Boundaries thereof will easily be descried: And indeed, the generals that are expressed, are a sufficient indication thereunto. His Majesty's Declaration concerning Ecclesiastical Affairs, hath mentioned particular Concessions on both sides, and that Harmony of Affections therein, He calls excellent Foundations to build upon. The Moderation and Indulgence there specified, would do the work; I mean not so as if all Dissenters would instantly be thereby brought in; but that our wide breach would presently be healed in great part, and be in the surest way for a total and absolute healing; and so much would be gained at present, as might be able to conquer the remaining Difficulties.

The

The former *Discourse* had this position, That the Ends of Church-Discipline do not require a Constitution of narrower bounds, then things necessary to Faith and Life, and Godly Order in the Church. The *Answerer* saith, That *this Establishment is not enough for a Settlement, because it doth not secure the Peace.* And to shew the insufficiency thereof, he giveth two instances of Discord between the Parties; First, about *the Persons to whose Care the great things of Christianity should be intrusted to see them conveyed unto Posterity, whether they shall be a Single Person, or a Consistory, or each single Congregation.* Secondly, About *the means of conveying those things, the Worship of God, and the Circumstances thereof.* From hence he draws this Conclusion, *Therefore to preserve Peace among her Members, the Church had need to determine more then the great things of Christianity; and to injoyn more then what is barely necessary to Faith and Order.* Verily, it may much amuse one to think what that thing should be in the Ecclesiastical Polity, which is not necessary to Christian Faith and Life, and godly Order in the Church, and yet necessary to secure the Church's Peace. And if the aforesaid Instances of discord between the *Church of England* and the *Dissenters* are not necessary to Faith or Order, what reason can be rendred of the inexorable Imposition thereof, upon dissenting or doubting Consciences? Can it be necessary to the Church's Peace, to exclude or deprive men for such Differences in which neither Faith nor Order are concerned? Or is this the *Answerer's* meaning, That the Church's Peace consists in the exclusion of the *Nonconformists*; and that the necessary use of some Injunctions, stands in keeping them out; so that not their Conformity, but their Exclusion is the thing therby intended?

The Comprehension doth not suppose (as it is mis-reported) *That Presbytery should be permitted or encouraged.* All

intermed-

intermedling with the Form of Church-Government, was declined ; only the preſcribed Uniformity was conſidered. Beſides, for the exact *Presbyterial* Form to be comprehended in *Epiſcopacy*, is contradictory ; yet 'that ſomething of *Presbytery* ſhould be included in it, is not repugnant. And ſuch a Comprehenſion is approved in His Majeſty's aforeſaid Declaration. Likewiſe King *CHARLES* the Firſt, in His Diſcourſe touching the Differences between Himſelf and the Two Houſes, in this point, declares that *He is not againſt the managing of the Epiſcopal Preſidency in one man, by the joint Counſel and Conſent of many Presbyters; but that He had offered to reſtore it as a fit means to avoid thoſe errors, and corruptions and partialities which are incident to any one man; alſo to avoid Tyranny, which becomes no Chriſtians, leaſt of all Church-men.* But neither this nor the former Treatiſe, interpoſeth in this Matter, but leaves it to the Wiſdom of our Superiors.

The deſired Latitude leaves not the Concernments of Church or State *to the Ingenuity of Men*, nor caſts out any Injunctions that are means of Peace and Unity ; yea, or of that neceſſary Decency which the Apoſtle requires ; only of Rites and Opinions long diſputed, it would take in no more then needs muſt ; and not meerly becauſe they have been long diſputed, but becauſe they are alſo of little value, (and here confeſſed not to be neceſſary to Faith and Order) yet are matters of endleſs Controverſie in this Church, and occaſions of great ſeparation from it.

It being aſſerted, That the indiſputable Truths of Faith, and the indiſpenſable Duties of Life, are the main Object of Church-Diſcipline, the *Anſwerer* demands, *What are thoſe indiſputable Truths, ſince there is ſcarce any Truth of Faith that hath not been diſputed againſt ?* What manner of arguing is this? Becauſe All Truths have been diſputed, doth it follow, that there are no indiſputable Truths? That

is

is called Indisputable, that cannot reasonably or justly be disputed, though men of corrupt minds, and reprobate concerning the Faith, will call the greatest Truths in question, and resist the clearest Evidence. When the Apostle mentions matters of doubtful disputations, he implies there be matters that are indubitable.

SECT. XII.

Of acquiescence in the Commands of Superiors, and the proper matter of their Injunctions.

IN the former Treatise this Argument was used. The Church doth not claim an Infallibility, therefore she cannot settle the Conscience by her sole Warrant, but still leaves room for doubting. The *Answerer* makes this to be either a piece of ignorance, or *of portentous malice*, and an Assertion *that would disturb all Government both in Families and in the State, that would confound all Society, and extirpate Faith and Justice from among the sons of men.* But this his strange Inference rather is portentous. That the Church cannot settle the Conscience by her sole Warrant, is it not a Principle maintained by all *Protestants* in opposition to the *Popish* implicit Faith, and blind Obedience? But is this person consistent with himself? For after he hath a while expatiated in his imaginary hideous Consequences, he comes himself to deny that the Church bindeth the Conscience by her own Authority. And yet it is a lesser thing to *bind* the Conscience, than to *settle it, and leave no room for doubting.* For Conscience may be obliged, when it is not setled. And if the Church cannot oblige, doubtless she cannot settle the Conscience by her sole Authority. How then could a man of reason draw such hideous Inferences from that Position? If I may give way to conjectures, I suspect that he might take check at the word *Infallibility*, by

which

which I intend no more then Infallible Direction; and I fear not to own this Affertion, That whofoever have not Infallible Direction, or the certain affiftance of an Infallible Guide, fo as to be exempted from all error in what they propound for Belief or Practice, cannot fettle the Confcience by their fole warrant.

I ftill aver, That in prefcribed Forms and Rites of Religion, the Confcience that doth its office, will interpofe and concern it felf. And it is matter of aftonifhment that a Learned *Proteftant* fhould fay, this Pofition muft needs be falfe. For Confcience guided by the fear of God, will ufe all juft means to difcern his Will, and cannot refign it felf to the dictates of men in the points of Divine Worfhip. If the Judgment of Difcerning, which makes men differ from Brutes, be to be exercifed in any cafe, it is chiefly requifite in thefe matters wherein the Glory of God, and the Saving of the Soul is fo much concerned.

It is granted, That to maintain Peace and Unity in the Church, and to be obedient to the Higher Powers in thofe things which are proper matter for their Commands, are moft ftrictly injoined Duties. But the Injunctions here confidered (though to the Impofers they are but things Indifferent, that is, neither Commanded nor Forbidden of God)in the Confciences of Diffenters, are Unlawful. To inftance in fome controverted Ceremonies, They think that God hath determined againft them, though not in particular, yet in the general Prohibition of all uncommanded Worfhip. And they reply, *Whether it be right in the fight of God to hearken unto men more then unto God, judg ye.* To reftrain that of the Apoftle, *He that doubts is damned if he eat,* only to things wherein the Church hath not interpofed her Authority, is a falfe glofs, and a begging of the Queftion. What human Authority can warrant any one to put in practice an unlawful or fufpected Action, or to make profeffion

feſſion of a known or ſuſpected Falſhood ? As concerning the Rights of Superiors , it is the Church's Duty and
Honour to teach and command her Children to do whatſoever Chriſt hath commanded. And it is the chiefeſt Glory,
and moſt proper Work of the Magiſtrate, who is Gods Mi-
niſter and Vicegerent,to be *cuſtos & vindex utriuſq; Tabulæ*,
To incourage and inforce Obedience to the Divine Laws,
whether written in the Bible, or imprinted in our Nature;
and in ſubſerviency thereunto , to have power to determine ſuch things as are requiſite in the general , but in the
particulars are left undetermined of God, and are to be ordered by Human Prudence, according to the Light of Nature, and the general Rules of Gods Word. But things indifferent in their nature, and either offenſive in their uſe, or
needleſs and ſuperfluous , are not worthy to be made *the
proper matter of his Commands*. It is a grave and weighty
ſaying of a Learned man (of whatſoever Perſwaſion he
were) " If the ſpecial Guides and Paſtors of the Church,
" would be a little ſparing of incumbring Churches with
" ſuperfluities,or not over-rigid,either in reviving obſolete
" Cuſtoms,or impoſing new,there would be far leſs cauſe of
" Schiſm and Superſtition ; and all the inconvenience that
" were likely to enſue, would be but this , That in ſo do-
" ing they ſhould yeeld a little to the imbecillity of their
" Inferiors; a thing which St. *Paul* would never have refu-
" ſed to do.

SECT. XIII.

*Of the alledged Reaſons of the Eccleſiaſtical Injunctions in
the beginning of the Reformation.*

THE *Anſwerer* relates at large the proceeding of this
Church in the beginning of the Reformation. The
ſum of the Relation is , *That there being Two ſorts of men,*
one

one that thought it a great matter of Conscience to depart from the least Ceremony, they were so addicted to their old Customs; the other so new-fangled, that they would innovate all things, and nothing would satisfie them but that which was new; It was necessary for the Church to interpose for Peace sake, and casting off neither Party, to please each to their edification; and also to injoyn some things to the common observance of all, and therefore she took away the excessive multitude of Ceremonies, as those that were dark, and abused to Superstition and Covetousness, but retained those few that were for Decency, Discipline, and apt to stir up the dull mind of man to the remembrance of his duty to God. We have good warrant to call in question the truth of his Narration in things of the greatest weight. First, It is not true that *the Party that were for Ceremonies, comprehended all those who staid at home, and did not flye in the time of* Queen Mary's *Persecution.* For such as dissented from the Ceremonies in the time of that Persecution, had their Assemblies for the Worship of God in this Land, and indured among others, in that Fiery Trial. And we can find but little zeal in the Martyrs of those days for this kind of Conformity. Likewise it is not true *that the Party that were against Ceremonies, were but small, as being but some few of those that fled beyond Sea:* There is clear evidence to the contrary. An Historian zealous for Conformity, even unto bitterness, reports in his *Ecclesia Restaurata*, That in the beginning of Queen *Elizabeth's* Reign, many that were disaffected to *Episcopacy* and Ceremonies, were raised to great Preferments. Besides, those that were in Ecclesiastical Dignities, he observes, That the Queens Professor at *Oxford*, and the *Margaret* Professor in *Cambridg*, were among the *Nonconformists*. For the multitude of *Dissenters* in those dayes, there is a notable testimony of a Friend of *Prelacy*, in his Letter to Mr. *Richard Hooker*, about the writing of his *Ecclesiastical Polity*,

in

in thefe words: *It may be remembred, that at the firft the greateft part of the Learned in the Land, were either eagerly affeded, or favourably inclined to that way; the Books then written, favoured for the moft part, of the Difciplinary ftile; it founded every where in the Pulpits, and in the common phrafe of mens fpeech; and the contrary Part began to fear they had taken a wrong courfe.*

There is as little Truth and Juftice in that report, *That the Party that were againft Ceremonies, caufed the Troubles at* Frankford, *and brought a Difhonor to the Reformation, and Infamy upon our Nation.* The *Englifh* Congregation at *Frankford*, was fetled after the Difcipline of the Foreign Reformed Churches, and enjoyed much Peace, till certain eminent men, zealous of the *Englifh* Forms and Rites, came among them, and by a high hand brought in the Liturgy, and brake them to pieces, and forced away the Minifters, and thofe Members that were in the firft forming and fetling of that Church. Afterward, they that remained and received the Liturgy, continued not long in unity, but in a fhort time an incurable and fcandalous Schifm brake out between the Paftor, and almoft the whole Congregation.

Laftly, There is a great miftake in the main bufinefs of the Narrative, in reprefenting things as fetled by the Church of *England* in the beginning of the Queen's Reign, to pleafe each Party in the abolifhing of fome, and the retaining of other Ceremonies: Whereas at the reviving the Reformation at that time, the Ceremonies then abolifhed were offenfive to all Proteftants, and nothing appears to be done in favour of the *Anticeremonial* Party, about the points in difference. But things were carried to a greater height againft their Way, than in King *Edward's* time, whofe Reformation was thought to incline more to that which was afterwards called *Puritanifm.* For which

caufe

caufe the Hiftorian before mentioned , hath written , *That that King being ill principled, his Death was no infelicity to the Church of England.* The truth of the matter is, That in the firft Times of the Queen , whofe Reign was to be founded in the Proteftant Religion , the Wifdom of the State intended chiefly the bringing over of the whole Body of the People , and to fettle them in that Profeffion; and therefore thought fit to make no more alteration from their old Forms, then was neceffary to be made. Care was taken, that no part of the Liturgy might be offenfive to the *Papifts* , and they accordingly reforted to our Divine Service for the firft Ten years. Alfo the retaining of the Ceremonies, was a matter of condefcention to the *Popifh* Party, the State thereby teftifying how far they would ftoop to gain them, by yeelding as far as they might in their own Way. Now long Experience hath fhewed , That what was done with refpect to the Peace of former Times, and reconciling of *Papifts* to *Proteftants*, is become an occafion of dividing *Proteftants* from one another , without hope of converting *Papifts*.

S E C T. XIV.

The alledged Reafons , why the Ceremonies are not to be taken away, Examined.

Divers Reafons are alledged to prove a continued neceffity for thefe Ceremonies, as, *Becaufe they that are for the Church , are unwilling to have them taken away: To revoke them, is to comply with thofe that will never be fatisfied: Imputations have been laid upon the Things injoyned, as* Antichriftian, Idolatrous, Superftitious: *A Warr was undertook to remove them: And it is a reproach to the Church, whofe Foundation is upon the Truth, to be various.* Hereunto we make anfwer: Whofoever delight in the ufe of the

Cere-

Ceremonies, may enjoy their liberty; but let it suffice them to use it, without ▪ying a stumbling-block before others, or intangling their Consciences, or hindring all of a contrary Perswasion from the Ministry, from teaching School, yea, and from taking any Academical Degree. With what sobernefs can it be said, the *Diſſenters* will never be satisfied, when hitherto they were never tryed with any Relaxation or Indulgence, although they have given evident proofs of their unfeigned deſires of Accommodation? They do indeed esteem the Ceremonies an exceſs in the Worſhip of God; but ſuppoſe that ſome have been immoderate in diſparaging thoſe Rituals; on the other hand, ſhall their value be ſo inhanſed, as to be thought more worth then the Church's Unity, and the exerciſe of mutual Charity among its Members? May not the Church ſalve her Honour, by declaring, That in remitting theſe Injunctions, ſhe meerly yeelds to the infirmity of weak Conſciences? As St. *Paul* declared concerning abſtaining from meats, who had as much power to make a Canon, as any ſort or number of Eccleſiaſtical perſons can now pretend unto. As concerning the late Warr, it is eaſier ſaid then proved, That it was undertaken to remove the Ceremonies; and it was not ſo declared by thoſe that managed it. But if it were ſo indeed, as it is here ſuggeſted, let this Argument be well weighed, A dreadful Warr that had a diſmal iſſue, was undertaken to remove certain Ceremonies that at the beſt are but indifferent, therefore let them never be removed, but ſtill inforced to the uttermoſt upon Conſciences that diſallow them. As for the reproach of the Church by the appearance of being various, we conceive the controverted Ceremonies are no Foundation of the Church of *England*, nor any ſubſtantial part of her Religion, and do therefore hope, that ſome Indulgence therein will not fix upon her any brand of Inconſtancy.

E   It

It is objected, That the *Popish* Priests would hereby take advantage. It seems then, that   eater care must be taken that the *Papists*, who are implacable Adversaries, be not offended, then that many thousand honestly minded *Protestants* should be relieved. But the strangest Reason comes up last. *Dissentions about things indifferent, have necessitated the Church to make these Injunctions*: That is, say the things are but indifferent, yet great dissentions have risen about them, and are like to continue without end ; therefore the Church hath been necessitated to impose them with great severity upon multitudes who esteem them unlawful, and all for this end, That dissentions may be removed. We are astonished at this Argument from the Pen of a Learned man. The truth is, these alledged Reasons have more of Animosity in them, then of Equity, Charity, or good Advice. Indeed the Apostle saith, *Mark those that cause divisions and offences contrary to the Doctrine that ye have received*; but he doth not so brand those that scruple unwritten Traditions, and needless Ceremonies, but adhere to the intire Doctrine of Christ, and all Divine Institutions.

SECT. XV.

Of the diversity of Opinion and Practice already permitted in the Church of England.

THE Moderation of the Church of *England* in the Articles of *Predestination*, *Divine Grace*, and *Free-will*, being urged against the rigorous imposition of the controverted Orders and Ceremonies, this Answer is made, *That the case is not the same, for that those points are so full of difficulty, that they, and questions of that nature, have been matter of dispute in all Ages, and in all Religions ; but about the Orders and Ceremonies, this is the only thing to be resolved, Whether the Church hath power to injoin an indifferent Ceremony?*

mony? But there is no such difference in the case. The Question of things Indifferent, hath been mistaken for the *Grand Case* of the *Nonconformists*; for those points which are the main reason and matter of their inconformity, are by them accounted not indifferent, but unlawful, and therefore not to be admitted in their practice, till their Consciences be better satisfied. And it is not irrational to think, that serious doubtings may arise in sober minds about some parts of the injoyned Uniformity, and particularly, about those Ceremonies which seem to draw near to the significancy and moral efficacy of Sacraments, and thereupon may appear to some not as meer circumstances, but as parts of Divine Worship, and their Consciences may be struck with Terror by the sense of God's Jealousie about any instituted Worship which Himself hath not prescribed. Moreover, these Orders and Ceremonies have been matters of dispute in all times since the beginning of *Protestant* Reformation. But under the degenerate state of the Christian Churches, by the great Apostacy of the later times, there could be no occasion of disputing these things, when Will-worship was generally exalted, and the grossest Idolatries had prevailed.

I question the truth of that Assertion, *That the Dissenters cannot name one Church besides ours, in which there was a Schism made for a Ceremony.* For a great Rent was made in the Christian Church throughout the World, about a Ceremony, or as small a matter, to wit, the time of celebrating the Feast of *Easter*. But whensoever a Schism is made, let them that cause it, look to it, and lay it to heart. *Wo to the world because of offences, and wo to that man by whom the offence cometh.* But we still insist upon this Argument, That these Rites being at the best but indifferent in the opinion of the Imposers, the observation of them cannot in reason be esteemed of such importance to the sub-

stance

ſtance of Religion, as the different Opinions about the Articles aforeſaid are. And who knows not with what animoſity and vehemence the Parties that are called *Arminian* and *Antiarminian*, have fought againſt one another; and what dreadful and deſtructiveConſequences they pretend to draw from each others Opinions? Now put caſe the more prevalent Party in the Church of *England* ſhould go about to determine thoſe Controverſies on the one ſide, or the other, (and truly they were ſometimes determined by a Synod in His Majeſty's Dominions, namely by that of *Dublin* in the year 1615, alſo by the greateſt Prelates, and moſt eminent Doctors in *England*, in the *Lambeth-Articles*; and what hath been, may again come to paſs) would not that ſide againſt whom the Deciſion paſſeth, be ready to cry out of Oppreſſion? Yea, how great a Rent would be made by it through the whole Fabrick of this Church? Furthermore, in Ceremonies publikely uſed, and matters of open practice, the Church of *England* hath thought good to indulge *Diſſents*, as in that of bowing toward the Altar, or the Eaſt, unleſs it be required by the local Statutes of particular Societies. And in this the Sons of the Church do bear with one another, according to the direction of the Canons made in the year 1640. Unto which may be added, That the Mode of Worſhip in Cathedrals, is much different from that in Parochial Churches. Likewiſe ſome Miniſters before their Sermon uſe a Prayer of their own conceiving; others onely (as the phraſe is) bid Prayer. If theſe and other Varieties, be no reproach to our Church, will it reproach her to ſuffer one to Officiate with a Surpliſs, and another without it?

SECT.

SECT. XVI.

Men differently perfwaded in the prefent Controverfies, may live together in Peace.

IT is no vain fpeculation, *to think we may have peace, if men perfwaded in their Confciences that the controverted Ceremonies are fuperftitious, or at the beft but Trifles, and that the Liturgy and Ecclefiaftical Polity, need fome Reformation, fhould be joined with men far otherwife perfwaded.* And the preferving of Peace in that cafe, doth not fuppofe or require *that all thefe differently perfwaded men, will be wife on both fides to content themfelves with their own opinions :* But it fuppofeth the State, and the chief Guides of the Church, to be wife, (as it is always requifite they fhould be) and that many of Reputation and Eminency on both fides, will be prudent and temperate, and examples of Moderation to others, (and not to fuppofe this is to difparage and debafe our prefent Age) but above all, it fuppofeth the Publike Conftitution fo well ftated and fetled, as to be able to curb the Imprudent and Unfober, and to encourage the Modeft and Well-advifed.

Surely all Diffenters upon Confcience, *will not be prevailed with by the fame Confcience, to endeavour the propagation of their own way in thefe differences, to the depreffion of others.* If fome offer to difturb the Peace, can no Rule of Government reftrain them ? It is a deplorable cafe indeed, if there be no remedy but for thofe that are favoured by the Higher Powers, utterly to exclude and reject thofe that want the like favour and countenance.

At this day the Church of *England* by Her prefent Latitude, or at leaft Connivence, keeps peace among Her Sons of fuch different Perfwafions, as formerly ftirred up great Diffentions in this Church. Who is ignorant of the Con-

Contentions raised about the *Arminian* Controversies in
the several Reigns of Queen *Elizabeth*, King *James*, and
King *Charles* the First? But in the present Times, the mutual forbearance on both sides, but chiefly the Church's
Prudence, hath lay'd asleep those Controversies; whereas
if one side presuming upon its Power and Prevalency,
should go about (as formerly) to decry and depress the
other, and to advance and magnifie themselves, and ingross
the Preferments, doubtless the like flames would break
out again. For there is a great dislike and abhorrency
setled at the Heart-root of both these Parties against
each others Opinions; and a sutable occasion would soon
draw it out to an open Contestation. Now it the Church's
Peace and Unity be already maintained in such seemingly
dangerous diversity of Opinion among her Members and
Officers, and those not of the meanest rank, why should
her Prudence and Polity be suspected as insufficient to
maintain Unity and Peace in the indulging of the differently perswaded in the now disputed Rites and Opinions?

S E C T. XVII.

*Of DISSENTERS of Narrower Principles, and of
TOLERATION.*

THE Latitude discoursed in the former Treatise, is un-
justly impeached, as providing onely for the *Presby-*
terians, and relinquishing all other Dissenters; for it com-
prehends within the Establishment, those of all sorts that
are of Principles congruous to stated Order in the Church;
so that no sort is excluded, whose Principles make them
capable. And was this Capacity any where restrained to
the *Presbyterians*? Some *Nonconformists* are for Moderated
Episcopacy, after the form of the Ancient Churches; and
divers

divers others, as to particular forms of Government, are *Latitudinarians*; and others there are besides these, who would live peaceably under the present Hierarchy, might they be spared from the personal profession or practice of some things which they think unlawful or doubtful.

Moreover, beyond the Established Order, the Latitude includes a Toleration for those that are of sound Faith, and good Life, but have taken up some Principles of Church-Government less congruous to National Settlement. I cannot yeeld to that position, *That only Necessity can give colour to Toleration, for that it is by the confession of all, one of those things that are not good in their nature.* I suppose that Christians bearing with one another in toleral differences, *is a branch of Brotherly Love*; and therefore Charity, as well as Necessity, may plead for this Way of Indulgence.

But it is objected, *That we want an instance of the safety of Toleration, in any Nation where the Supreme Governour had not a standing Army to circumscribe and confine the Heats of Dissenters in Religion, to their own breasts, and keep off the destructive Effects of Schism.*

Let me reply, That this Maxime, That no Toleration of Dissenters, howsoever regulated, can be safely granted by the Supreme Governour that hath not a standing Army, makes little for the Safety and Liberty of true Religion. The *Protestants* that live under the Princes of the *Roman* Faith, are little beholding to one that publisheth to the World, That those Princes can with safety tolerate them no longer then they keep up a standing Army to keep off the destructive effects of that which they call Schism. One may see by this and other instances, what bias the Judgment hath, by the Zeal of a Party, and how it is brought to assert such things as may expose the true Religion to the danger of Suppression or Extirpation in many Countries.

But

But hath the *French* King less assurance of the Loyalty of His *Protestant* Subjects, then of the *Roman-Catholicks*? Would a Necessity be laid upon Him to maintain constant Forces to keep the *Protestants* in obedience, when he could rule the rest of his People without such Terror? Or is Toleration the reason of a standing Army in the United Provinces of the *Netherlands*? In this Latitude no other Toleration is pleaded for, then what can be made safe and secure by the ordinary ways of Legal Government.

Both Duty and Interest obligeth all sorts to proceed as far as it is possible in complying with their Superiors; and if the uncontrolable Power of Conscience inforce them to lye without the Pale of the Established Order, they should deem that Exclusion their great Unhappiness. But so it is, that Prudent and Pious men may be of exceeding Narrow Principles about Church-Order and Fellowship. Christian Charity pleadeth for Indulgence towards them; and we hope Political Prudence doth not gainsay it. For although their Way may fall far short of setling a Nation, yet they may have Spirits and Principles very consistent with Publike Tranquility. And their Indulgence may be obtained by a good Understanding and Confidence between Them and the Higher Powers, the Clemency of the One shewing Favour in that extent which the Publike Order may safely tolerate; and the Humility and Discretion of the Other, causing them to prise the Favour, and to use it rightly. That such Condescention and Clemency should be used on the One side, and such Humility and Modesty on the Other, why should it seem impossible? For the One may see, that by granting some Limited Liberty, the Protection of Christs Flock, and the Satisfaction of well-minded Subjects may become more Universal: And the Other may likewise see, that a smaller Party, and those of Narrow Principles, are of

them-

themſelves in no wiſe proportionable to the State of this
Nation; and therefore that they cannot well ſubſiſt, but
in conjunction with, and ſubordination unto an Eſtabliſhment more commenſurate to the whole Body of the People.
This neceſſary Subordination, may beget a mutual Confidence and Security. If it be ſaid, The Tolerated Party
may become Dangerous or Suſpected, it is always ſuppo-
ſed that they ſtand by their Good Behaviour, and the
Rulers Favour. But they are not like to prove Dangerous, if the Eſtabliſhment be large enough. For the Nar-
rowneſs thereof makes the *Diſſenters* numerous, and ſtill
encreaſeth their Number.

S E C T. XVIII.

*It is the Intereſt of the NONCONFORMISTS to pre-
fer Comprehenſion before Toleration, where Conſcience
doth not gainſay.*

IF it can be made evident, That the *Nonconformiſts* ſhould
embrace a Comprehenſion as the ſureſt means of their
particular Good, it will conduce exceedingly to evince,
That the Favour of Rulers will not be in vain towards
them; and that their Petitions, Diſcourſes, and other In-
ſtances for Moderation, were not feigned, becauſe ground-
ed on their true Intereſt that cannot lye.

Were they united among themſelves, and did the Times
highly favour them, even then it were their Wiſdom not
to inſiſt too far upon their own Perſwaſions, but to comply
with ſuch moderate Order as is moſt paſſable in the Nation, (their Conſciences not gainſaying) much more doth
it now behove them, by Moderation and Submiſſion to
diſpoſe themſelves for the Favour of their Superiors.

They ſhould chuſe rather (if it be poſſible for them) to
be Comprehended in the Approved, then to be Tolerated

F

in

in a Severed Way. For there is not so much lost thereby in point of Liberty, but as much or more is gained in point of Safety.

It is a happiness to be secured from dangerous wanderings, perplexities, breaches, and manifold inconveniences, into which they may be led that are wholly left without the Line of the Established Order. Those persons that by their Wisdom and Learning can the better defend themselves from the aforesaid Evils in a severed State, cannot be ignorant how precipitate and unadvisable many of their Number may be, and not so easily to be governed by their more prudent Guides. Men of discerning and stable judgments, would do their uttermost to preserve the more inconsiderate people from falling into a full and absolute Separation from all Christian Societies that are not of their Perswasion. For they may easily apprehend into how great and dangerous Errors that *Vortex* may carry about those that fall into it.

They that are best able to govern themselves, do see most need of a Publike Government, and how necessary it is, that both People and Teachers be under the Regulation and Influence of Authority, for the avoiding of many and great Inconveniencies. And there are many and great Benefits, by being comprehended in the Approved Order, not otherwise to be obtained. Their Peace is better insured, their Influence is more diffusive, their Instances and Motions for the Common Good, will be more regarded. They have a larger scope for imploying their Masters Talent in the Publike Service of the Gospel, and they may speak with more Authority, and better success among all ranks and sorts of men, who will look upon them as theirs, when they hold their Publike Stations.

Unto all this may be added, That the Ancient *Nonconformists* earnestly opposed the Separation of the *Brownists*, and

and held communion with the Church of *England* in its Publike Worſhip.

And doubtleſs it is the Miniſters Intereſt, not to have their Subſiſtence by the Arbitrary Benevolence of the people, and ſo to live in continual dependance upon their mutable diſpoſitions for a Maintenance that is poor and low in compariſon of the Publike Encouragements. Hereby one may partly judg, whether Learned and Prudent men be *Nonconformiſts* by the pleaſure of their own will, or the conſtraining-force of Conſcience.

Now their Conſciences may be relieved, if they be not made perſonally to profeſs or practice any thing againſt the dictates thereof. And retaining their own private judgments, they may well hold to this Catholick Principle, That in a Church acknowledged to be ſound in Doctrine, and in the Subſtance or main Parts of Divine Worſhip, and not defective in any vital part of Chriſtian Religion, they are bound to bear with much which they take to be amiſs in others Practice, in which they do not perſonally bear a part themſelves,

As concerning a Form of Church-Government, and Rule of Diſcipline, Men that underſtand their own Intereſt, cannot for ſelf-ends (as they have been upbraided) court the Power of ſuch a Diſcipline as inevitably procures envy and ill-will, without any temporal profit or dignity. And if the Higher Powers will not admit ſuch a Form, (I deliver my own private judgment, without prejudice to other mens) this may tend to ſatisfie the Subjects Conſcience, That Eccleſiaſtical Government is neceſſarily more directed and ordered in the exerciſe thereof, by the Determinations of the Civil Magiſtrate, in places where the true Religion is maintained, then where it is perſecuted or diſregarded. And they that have received the Power, muſt anſwer to God for it : They that

F 2   are

are difcharged from it, fhall never account for that where-
of they have been bereaved.

S E C T. XIX.

*It behoves both the Comprehended and the Tolerated, to prefer
the common Interefl of Religion, and the fetling of the
Nation, before their own particular Perfwafions.*

AS thofe *Diffenters*, whofe Confciences will permit,
will beft comply with their own good, by entring
into the Eftablifhment, if a door be open for their accefs :
So they of Narrower Principles, that cannot enter into it,
will be fafeft within the Limits of fuch Indulgence as Authority would vouchfafe to grant them, with refpect to the
Common Good. Men of all Perfwafions fhould rather
chufe to be limited by Publike Rules, with mutual Confidence between their Governors and Themfelves, then to
be left to the liberty of their own Affections, upon terms
uncertain and unfecure.

Befides the Concernment of their own Peace, there is
this great Perfwafive, That this Advice is a compliance
with that ftate of things which will beft fatisfie and fettle the Nation, and maintain Reformed Religion againft
Popery, and Chriftianity againft Atheifm and Infidelity.

True *Englifhmen*, and Lovers of their dear Countrey,
which is impaired and reproached by thefe breaches, fhould
yeeld as much to its Wealth and Honour, as their Confciences can allow. Loyal Subjects and good Patriots fhould
confider what the Kingdom will bear, and prefer fuch
bounded Liberty of Comprehenfion and Indulgence, as
tends to Union, before a loofe, though larger Liberty,
that will keep the Breaches open, and the Minds of People unquiet and unfetled. And it is not of little moment
to mind this, That the high Concerns of Confcience cannot

not be better secured then in the Peace and Safety of the excellent Constitution of this Kingdom.

For the Amplitude of Reformed Religion, all true Protestants should promote an ample Establishment thereof, both for the incompassing of all that be found in that Profession, as also for the more capacious reception of those that may become Converts thereunto. And not onely the encrease and glory thereof, but its stability in these Dominions, is promoted by such an ample Establishment. Witness our great Defence against *Popery*, by the common zeal of all *Protestants* of the several Perswafions, for *Protestancy* in general. By this concurrent Zeal, the infolencies of the *Papists* have been repressed, and their Confidences defeated. Could the *Protestant Conformists* or *Nonconformists*, either of them upon their own single account, if one should exterminate, or utterly disable the other, be so well secured against *Popery*, as now they are by their common Interest? And to imagine by rigor to compel the depressed Party to incorporate with the Party advanced, so that one should acquire the Strength of both, would in the issue be found a great Error. By such proceeding, indeed, a Party may be wounded and broken, and rendred unserviceable to the common good, but shall never be gained as an addition of Strength to those who have so handled them. But an Accommodation would make both to be as one. And seeing in their present divided state, the concurrent Zeal of Both hath been so formidable, as to dash the hopes of the *Popish* Party, how much more in a state of Union, might their Strength increase against their common Adversaries! Wherefore, the One should open the Way, and the Other should readily come in upon just Terms. This should be the rather minded on both sides, because the Considerate *Nonconformists* will never promote their own Liberty by such ways and means as would bring in a Toleration

leration of *Popery*; yea, they would rather help to bear up the prefent Ecclefiaftical ftate, then that *Popery* fhould break in by *Anarchy*, or the Diffolution of all Church-Government.

Moreover, an ample, fixed ftate Ecclefiaftical, is neceffary to uphold and encreafe trueReligion, as well againft *Infidelity*, as againft *Popery*. The loofe part of theWorld would turn to a wearinefs and contempt of Divine Inftitutions, and Chriftianity it felf would be much endangered in a ftate of Ataxy and unfixednefs. By what ordinary means hath the Doctrine and Inftitution of Chrift been propagated and perpetuated in large Kingdoms and Nations, and in the Univerfe, but by incompaffing under its external Rule and Order, great Multitudes that may fall fhort of the Life and Power thereof. And it doth not root and fpread in any fort confiderable, in a Region, where the external Order is fet by the Rigid and Narrow Principles of a fmall Party, and the general Multitude lyes open as waft ground, for any to invade or occupy. Let confiderate men judg how much the ample ftate of a meer Orthodox Profeffion, is to be preferred before *Infidelity*, or *Popery*, or any other Sect of the Chriftian Name, that is Idolatrous or Heretical. There be few Converts to the Power of Godlinefs, from Infidelity or Popery, or any Herefie, but they are generally made out of the Mafs of People of an Orthodox Profeffion.

If it be the will of God that one muft fuffer for the Caufe of Religion, it is more for the Honour of Chriftianity to fuffer from Infidels, then from *Papifts*; likewife it is more for the Honour of Reformed Religion, to fuffer from *Papifts*, then from *Proteftants*. And if it were at ones own choice, One fhould much rather (*cæteris paribus*) fuffer in defence of the main Truths of *Chriftianity*, then for refufing a Ceremony, or for any other part of *Inconformity*.

formity. For this caufe a Union is fo defirable, that thefe Bitternefles, Reproaches and Scandals, might ceafe from among us.

Laftly, Whatfoever Enlargement we have granted by the Favour of our Lawful Superiors, we have it in the beft way, and a Blefling is in it.

SECT. XX.

EPISCOPACY will gain more by Moderation, then by Severity in thefe Differences.

THE *Anfwerer* enumerates many Reafons why *a Form of Church-Government fhould meet with many Diffi-culties in its return after a profcription of Twenty years*; and concludes *it muft be a Generation or two, not feven years, that can wear out all thofe Difficulties*. On the other fide he faith, *Presbytery languifhed almoft as foon as it had a being*, &c. I perceive *Presbytery* is a great Eye-fore. Per-adventure I may be reckoned a *Presbyterian*; and to fay the truth, I am not afhamed of their company that are commonly called by that Name; yet I have no pleafure in fuch Names of diftinction. I am of a *Perfwafion*, but not of a *Party*; and whatfoever my *Perfwafion* be, it is Moderate, Catholick and Pacifick. Neither my Defign nor my Principles engage me to maintain the *Presbyterial* Government. Neverthelefs I cannot but take notice with how little reafon the intrinfick Strength of *Prelacy*, or Weaknefs of *Presbytery*, is argued from the duration of the one and the other in this Kingdom. Had *Presbytery* the Strength of the Civil Power? Or was it ever formed in *England*? Was it not crufh'd while it was an *Embryo*, by the prevailing Potency of its Adverfaries? Look into thofe States where it hath been Eftablifhed, if you would judg aright concerning it. On the other hand, hath not *Prelacy*
had

had all the Strength of Law and Power engaged in its defence, by the Encouragements of Worldly Grandure for its
Favourers, and by Severities inflicted on its Impugners for
above Fourscore years? In which space of time, none
could appear against it without the hazard of utter undo-
ing, or great Suffering. And though it were thus born up,
not for Seven years, but almost a Century, yet we do not
find that it had worn out the Difficulties of those Times,
which were not so Many and Great as this Author reports
its present Difficulties to be, in its return after a proscripti-
on of Twenty years. But there is a more excellent and
surer Way, which, it is hoped, may attain to a happier End
in less time then a *Generation or two.* If the Distemper of
Minds were healed, and Unchristian Enmities laid aside,
then Moderation being sincerely begun, would hold on,
and make the Disagreeing Parties to be still more yeelding, and mutually obliging; those Provocations and Prejudices would then cease, by which they have been mutually alienated, and hurried into such Hostilities, and
they would not be tempted in their own Defence (as they
think) to strengthen themselves by Evil Advantages.

If *Episcopacy* yeeld to a Moderate Course, why should
any prudent *Dissenters* go about to molest it? For in so
doing they would but perpetuate their own trouble and
unquiet state, seeing that diversities of Opinions, and occasions of Discord are like to continue about Forms of
Church-Government, until Forms shall be no more. On
the other side, Why should the *Episcopal* Clergy dread
that Moderation that would render *Episcopacy* more generally inoffensive and acceptable, and put some end to the
hitherto uncessant struglings against it? Are they jealous
that the Structure of their Government may be weakned,
and at length dissolved? They might rather apprehend
it might gain Assistance and Reputation from many that

now

now either by conftraint and neceffity, or by provocation
and prejudice are made its Adverfaries. Who fo fearch-
eth to the root of the matter, fhall find, That not fo much
the *Species* of Government, nor the Forms that are ufed
as weightier matters, have been the chief ftumbling block,
and the occafions of the greateft difguft and averfation.
Neither the *Epifcopal* Office nor Habit, doth affright this
fort of People from hearing a Bifhop preach to their E-
dification.

The right and fure way to eftablifh *Epifcopacy* in a Land
where *Reformed Chriftianity* is eftablifhed, is not to urge
precife Conformity in Opinions and Orders, and doubtful things of meer human determination; but to encourage foundnefs in the Faith, Ability and Induftry in the
proper Work of the Miniftry, and a Converfation becom-
ing the Gofpel; and to difcourage Pluralities, Nonrefiden-
cies, Licentioufnefs and Idlenefs in all forts, who ferve not
Chrift, but themfelves, in their Sacred Functions, and
whofe End is onely to live in Pomp, Wealth and Pleafure.
Will the Church-Governors fay (as it hath been anfwer-
ed) *they are bound up by the Laws; and if Patrons prefent
unworthy perfons which have the Qualifications the Law requires, the Bifhops muft not reject them; nor can they turn
them out at their pleafure, but muft give an account to the
Laws.* To this I reply, If the Admiffion and Permiffion
of unworthy Minifters, comes to pafs not by the Bifhops
Adminiftration, but by the defectivenefs of the Laws, why
hath not their Zeal excited them in the fpace of fo many
years, and feveral Princes Reigns, to endeavour the ob-
taining of Laws effectual on that behalf, as it hath to pro-
cure and make, from time to time, ftricter and ftricter Injunctions about Conformity and Ceremonies? For we
know no reafon why as full and vigorous Laws may not
be made againft Ignorant, Negligent and Scandalous Mi-

G   nifters,

nifters, as againft *Nonconformifts.* Confcience, Honour and
Safety, obligeth the *Epifcopal* Clergy to turn the edg of
their Difcipline the right way, and to fhew its energy
and vigor, not about Ceremonies, but the great and
weighty matters of Chriftian Religion. And I believe that
many worthy Minifters of the *Church of England,* are fo
perfwaded. Wherefore, in the former Difcourfe I caft no
evil reflection upon the *Latitudinarians,* or any moderate
perfons; nor reprefented them *as conforming not fincerely,
and as becomes the Minifters of Chrift.* They may fincerely,
according to their Principles, fubmit to thefe Impofitions,
and yet not like the Impofing. The expreffion of their
lukewarmnefs in Conformity, fignified no more but this,
That they fet a rate upon thefe Matters according to the
value, and that they bear but an indifferent refpect to things
that at the beft are but indifferent.

It is objected againft me, That *having provided a place
of reft for my felf and my Party, in the ftated Order, I am
little follicitous for others.* I do here folemnly profefs, That
I am chiefly follicitous for the Tranquility and Reft of a
troubled Nation. As for my own Concernment, my Deprivation is an Affliction to me; and I would do any thing
that were not fin to me, to recover the liberty of my publike Service in the Church: But if it cannot be, I fubmit
to His good pleafure, by whofe determinate Counfel all
things are brought to pafs, and am contented to remain a
Silenced Sufferer *for Confcience towards God.* Yea, I fhould
much rejoice in fuch Enlargement of the Publike Rule, as
might give a fafe entrance to others, though I my felf by
fome invincible ftrictnefs of Apprehenfion, fhould remain
excluded; for I have no Faction to uphold, and by others
Gain I am nothing leffened. And in my opinion, it will be no
dividing of the *Nonconformifts,* or weakning of their Intereft, if a part of them might clofe with the Approved
Order

Order of the Nation, enlarged to the latitude of their judgments, when others of ſtreighter judgments are left without. Indeed, if they were a Faction, they might loſe or leſſen themſelves hereby: But Reformed Chriſtianity is their Grand Intereſt, and their main Cauſe lyes not in any avowed difference of Doctrines between them and the *Epiſcopal Proteſtants*, nor in any Secular Advantages to hold to themſelves in a divided ſtate, but in the Advancement of Gods Kingdom by the encreaſe of true Chriſtian Faith and Piety.

The *Anſwerer* hath uſed many hard ſpeeches againſt me, and charged me with Malice in divers paſſages, which I anſwer not in particular, becauſe the innocence and inoffenſiveneſs of my words will clear it ſelf; and becauſe I would not make this *Diſcourſe* tedious, by replying to things impertinent to the main ſcope. It ſhall ſuffice me to add, That I have written theſe things, as knowing that *the Judg ſtandeth before the Dore.*

FINIS.

The Contents.